Implementing an Integrated Management System (IMS)

The strategic approach

Implementing an Integrated Management System (IMS)

The strategic approach

ALAN FIELD

IT Governance Publishing

IT Governance Publishing Ltd
Unit 3, Clive Court
Bartholomew's Walk
Cambridgeshire Business Park
Ely, Cambridgeshire
CB7 4EA
United Kingdom
www.itgovernancepublishing.co.uk

© Alan Field 2019

The author has asserted the rights of the author under the Copyright, Designs and Patents Act, 1988, to be identified as the author of this work.

First published in the United Kingdom in 2019 by IT Governance Publishing.

ISBN 978-1-78778-124-5

ACKNOWLEDGEMENTS

I would like to thank Chris Achillea; UK Head of Compliance at his current workplace, and Chris Wright; director of Wright-Canda consulting, for their time and helpful comments during the review process.

ABOUT THE AUTHOR

Alan Field, MA, LL.B (Hons), PgC, MCQI CQP, MIIRSM, GIFireE, is a chartered quality professional, an IRCA registered lead auditor and member of The Society of Authors.

Alan has particular expertise in auditing and third-party assessing anti-bribery management systems (ABMSs) to ISO 37001 and BS 10500 requirements, and counter-fraud systems in the public sector to ISO 9001 requirements. He has many years' experience with quality and integrated management systems in the property, engineering, legal and financial sectors. Alan also has experience in auditing, assessment and gap analysis roles within the project management sector.

CONTENTS

INTRODUCTION

This pocket guide is a strategic overview of what an integrated management system (IMS) is, and the leadership implications of implementing one. It explains what an IMS can be and how it can help an organisation achieve its goals, with the key concepts that underpin it.

What an IMS actually *is* varies from organisation to organisation, so this pocket guide is aimed at readers who are either interested in or actively involved with achieving what their IMS will become and the strategic decisions to be made.

The guide is not a detailed discussion of the standards and their requirements that could create an IMS. ITGP produces a number of excellent guides on standards such as ISO 9001:2015[1] and ISO 14001:2015[2], which detail what these standards require and how they can be useful to an organisation.

Like the mythical creature Cerberus, an IMS is often seen as a many-headed beast to confront; in fact, with strategic planning the meeting can be the reverse. Ongoing contact can be a lot friendlier and more positive when the various approaches to, and interpretations of an IMS, are understood upfront.

A 'bottom-up' implementation of an IMS might be possible in some smaller organisations, but with leadership involvement from day one an IMS journey will be more focused. This guide approaches implementation in a leadership-driven way.

If key planning decisions are not taken at the outset, the IMS journey can become unnecessarily slow or even misdirected. This book not only helps that journey but also – just as importantly – helps interpret needs to be decided upfront.

---

[1] *www.itgovernancepublishing.co.uk/product/iso-9001-2015*.

[2] *www.itgovernancepublishing.co.uk/product/iso-14001-step-by-step-a-practical-guide*.

This is also why this guide explores the ideas and concepts that an IMS is based upon. This is for two reasons:

1. All these concepts can be interpreted by each organisation and each leadership team for their own circumstances and goals; and
2. A lot of the practical issues involved with integrating operational processes are informed by the risk and opportunities-based objectives.

After all, organisations that have adopted Standards such as ISO 27001:2013 or ISO 9001:2015 are already doing this to a greater and lesser extent, so integration will be more straightforward at every level if these matters are clear from the outset. Shortcuts in the strategic process will usually prove a false promise.

As figure 1 will show, the number of management systems that can be integrated is almost exhaustive. Many organisations start with ISO 9001:2015 and then integrate it with, say, ISO 14001:2015, but, as we will discuss later, an IMS can develop without ISO standards and there is no minimum or maximum that can be integrated. However, the decision to integrate only some standards might be due to differences in management responsibility or sometimes, areas such as information security, require different risk treatments to say, quality or environmental management.

In broad terms, risk and opportunities cross both processes and scenarios. While much has been written about how an IMS can reduce bureaucracy and duplication, the real benefit can come from minimising risks and maximising opportunities.

Also, an IMS isn't the goal in itself; it is a servant – albeit a very important one – to what the organisation is attempting to achieve be it financial, reputational, ethical or technical objectives or of course, meeting stakeholder expectations.

What is an IMS?

In broad terms, an IMS is an integration of all an organisation's processes and systems working under – and towards – one set of policies and objectives. In other words, risk and opportunities are no longer managed in silos within the organisation, but instead with one unified, or integrated, approach from the leadership team.

Figure 1: An example of standards that can be incorporated into an IMS

In reality, an IMS is often an ongoing integration of the management systems that currently support the organisation. Creating an IMS isn't like flicking a switch. Rarely is it achieved by slavishly sticking to one particular system or approach; it will often be influenced by the good, the bad and occasionally the rather ugly aspects of the different management systems that make up the proposed or new IMS.

These might include a quality management system (QMS), an environmental management system (EMS), an occupational health and safety management system (OHSMS), business continuity management system (BCMS) and sometimes an information security management system (ISMS). Even more common is that just two or three of these systems will be integrated together under one set of objectives and leadership responsibilities.

Before looking at this in more detail, it is worth answering a question that is often asked: what is the difference between an integrated and combined management system?

The combined approach reflects an organisation that prefers to operate its risk management system in silos or distinct functional responsibilities but where there is a level of integration or common systems across some elements. For example, the board director responsible for an OHSMS may be different to the board director responsible for the EMS, but there may be some integrated elements, e.g. objectives, risk assessments, documented information, internal audit processes, or any combination of these.

Many an IMS will begin as a combined system that eventually becomes integrated, as all the elements of a management system become fused. Indeed, a management system assessor will often need to judge if a management system has really been integrated – rather than just combined – by how far a combined system has achieved integration.

So, the real distinction between an integrated and a combined approach is not binary – integration is, indeed, a journey and it may take time to fully achieve, and some resources will need to be devoted to it. An organisation needs to explicitly decide if it wants to do this – it is not just a nice thing to have.

The decision to integrate

A newly formed organisation may decide to have an IMS. However, many readers will already be working for or with organisations that have a variety of approaches to management systems. This might range from a well-resourced combined system to, possibly, very little in the way of systems at all.

So, the decision to implement an IMS remains a strategic objective. This could be motivated by the need to minimise risk; improve safety or environmental performance for contractual or reputational enhancement; provide greater efficiency in terms of cost; or simplify administrative processes or functional structures.

Another aim of an IMS might be to simplify the monitoring and measurement processes in place. This will particularly appeal to organisations where Lean or Six Sigma-type processes are used (be it formally or just as an influence). This is because a more integrated approach to efficiency is often seen as a way to cut across process and functionality.

If a leadership team says its motive for implanting an IMS is continual improvement, the exact improvements being sought need to be defined upfront, even if these strategic goal(s) evolve into rather different priorities or enhancements. The reason is simple to state but not so easy to achieve: the strategic goal(s) are the compass for the journey. Without them, resources can be diverted into implementing an IMS that could be supporting unnecessary detours, rather than supporting the strategic goals.

CHAPTER 1: BENEFITS OF AN IMS

Prevents duplication of effort

Many organisations will find that when integrating all or most of their existing management system's programmes (be these quality, information security, health and safety, and others), they will all have their functional processes and teams. An IMS can fuse these together, avoiding duplication in processes, procedures and functional middle-management time.

Efficient use of senior management time

Risk and opportunities can be looked at more strategically with an IMS and there is less duplication of time, money and effort in leadership governance. Monitoring and measurement processes for each of the management systems can be fused into more focused reporting, i.e. less time on considering multiple reports and less chance of key risk trends being missed in a mass of detail.

Uses resources to implement and manage systems more efficiently

While time and effort may be expended in creating the IMS, this can be more than recovered through the streamlining of systems and risk-based thinking once the IMS is achieved. Processes such as training and compliance auditing can be resourced on a process basis rather than individually resourcing different functional programmes.

The other key issue is that if an organisation is working in silos, there will be multiple demands for resources to support management systems. This can lead to tension, or competition for resources and attention at leadership level. For example, the quality and environmental management teams might compete for resources, but this will be based on their own siloed perceptions of risk-based priorities. If the organisation accepts they would benefit from a more holistic or strategic approach to risk and opportunities, the competition between such teams for resources is simply illogical and wasteful. Also, in the medium term, an IMS should create a greater sense of common priorities among the team(s) supporting the IMS, and less duplication of processes will also use finite resources more efficiently.

Reduces audit fatigue

Less siloed thinking leads to more integrated auditing, e.g. quality, health, safety and environmental management audit trails can be combined. Overall, less internal audit time may be necessary or, at least, the number of individual audits will certainly reduce. This can mean less disruption to day-to-day processes, and reduced 'audit fatigue' in some participants' minds.

Enables a united management approach

The above points show how an IMS often arises from looking critically at the silos within your organisation and asking if this is the most effective way of managing stakeholder expectations.

While silos are the most effective way for some organisations to manage affairs, the two tests are:

1. Are we using joined-up thinking, or are parts of the organisation working independently or even in inadvertent opposition?
2. Are we duplicating effort – could those duplicated resources be used for more productive outcomes?

If the answer is 'no' to either of these questions, the resources needed to create or evolve an IMS are almost certainly worth it.

Achieves more cost-effective certification

For larger organisations an IMS is likely to lead to less overall assessment time being required by the certification body (CB) concerned. Don't forget it is not just the assessment fees that form the true cost – it is the management time spent preparing and hosting the assessments, so any reduction in this has many benefits. Also, the assessment team is more likely to focus on the overall key risk and opportunities that the IMS is currently configured upon. This, in turn, can contribute towards continual improvement goals, rather than tick-box outcomes.

CHAPTER 2: TERMS AND DEFINITIONS

As outlined in the previous chapter, there are a number of concepts or guidelines that could help plan an IMS implementation and decide upon its strategic approach. Just as importantly, they can help define what the IMS policy and objectives can achieve.

We haven't discussed specifications such as PAS 99:2012 (a Publicly Available Specification for integrated management systems) because many organisations will be taking existing management systems and creating an IMS from them. While PAS 99 is an excellent tool, looking at Annex SL will provide more of a grounding in the principles behind the purpose of an IMS. If you look at the heading of PAS 99 after looking at Annex SL, the synergies are obvious.

The other reason for not looking too specifically at PAS 99 is organisations that are using European Foundation for Quality Management (EFQM) Excellence Model (but more from a quality management perspective – or using specifically or more broadly Lean or Six Sigma approaches, may find using Annex SL principles as a starting point more helpful in terms of understanding practical implications. The fundamental difference for Lean and Six Sigma readers is that there is more emphasis on risk management within Annex SL and metrics can be hard as well as soft – see chapter three. For EFQM readers there are a number of subtle differences with Annex SL. Yet in many ways the strategic part of Annex SL is not as wide as EFQM but, arguably, presents more emphasis on how risk-based strategy impacts on day-to-day organisational processes, rather than just the organisation's strategic direction.

In fact, readers may find their IMS planning is encouraged by taking a helicopter overview of how different management systems approach things – be it the ISO 9001 series, EFQM, Lean and Six Sigma. These, and many other proprietary approaches (e.g. COBIT 5®, for IT management, and Hazard Analysis and Critical Control Points (HACCP) for food safety) can be interpreted for a much wider business audience, i.e. they can provoke ideas and discussion about how risk is managed in any organisation. Sounds confusing, but in reality the similarities and differences can be surprisingly obvious when each organisation applies its own circumstances to these different approaches.

For example, HACCP is about food safety. However, whatever the processes are, HACCP can make you think about your own processes, which may have absolutely nothing to do with food safety. Consider how each stage of a process creates risks and how each stage of that process may then need different controls. These controls may be in isolation or form a series of controls as the process progresses.

Understanding risks on a stage-by-stage basis can also help identify opportunities, e.g. more efficient ways of doing things. Admittedly, in very broad terms HACCP is one example of how integration is about holistic thinking across processes and not just functional responsibilities. So, integration shows how a true process approach is about looking at the process itself, rather than the individual or functional aspects, e.g. many risks relate to archiving a file – from sourcing the paper the documents are prepared on, to the data protection issues of its long-term storage, and everything in between.

So, an IMS is really as much about developing efficient and risk-based processes as much as any management systems that support them – integrated or not. This is one strategic point to keep in mind in terms of outcomes being achieved.

Annex SL

In broad terms, Annex SL's high-level structure (HLS) does what it says on the tin. It means that all future assessable ISO standards will need to follow the high-level requirements outlined in Annex SL:

- Clause 1 – Scope
- Clause 2 – Normative references
- Clause 3 – Terms and definitions
- Clause 4 – Context of the organization
- Clause 5 – Leadership
- Clause 6 – Planning
- Clause 7 – Support
- Clause 8 – Operation
- Clause 9 – Performance evaluation
- Clause 10 – Improvement

As the International Organization for Standardization (ISO) says:

> Annex SL harmonizes structure, text and terms and definitions, while leaving the standards developers with the flexibility to integrate their specific technical topics and requirements.[3]

The British Standards Institution (BSI) and the American Society for Quality both have interesting discussions of what Annex SL means:

- *www.bsigroup.com/LocalFiles/nl-nl/iso-9001/BSI-Annex-SL-Whitepaper.pdf*

---

[3] *www.iso.org/news/2012/07/Ref1621.html*.

- *https://videos.asq.org/explaining-annex-sl-and-top-managements-new-roles*

However, Annex SL should be read as a document and not just consulted – even if the proposed IMS doesn't follow ISO standards. The approach taken with the HLS can assist with defining strategic ideas and might provoke other ideas within some organisations, e.g. is risk-based thinking the only approach to take with management systems? Or, just as likely, what does risk-based thinking mean to an organisation?

Annex SL assumes that continual improvement is the goal of every organisation because Annex SL regards the Plan-Do-Check-Act (PDCA) model as a core approach to process management. Annex SL also assumes that all management systems should be leadership led and managed and, finally, that risk-based thinking is used throughout the PDCA model.

Since 2012, many new versions of ISO standards – such as ISO 27001, ISO 9001 and ISO 14001 – have been issued incorporating Annex SL requirements. One intended output of this is that an organisation will find it more straightforward to create an integrated or, indeed, a combined management system as the HLS will be the same across all standards.

So, for example, an organisation with ISO 9001:2015 and ISO 14001:2015 will now be working to a common HLS even though both these standards have some very similar and rather different requirements. This should make devising a combined system and, possibly, an IMS more straightforward.

Leadership

Annex SL requires management systems to be leadership led. This was always the case with some alternative (or complementary) models to ISO standards, such as the EFQM Excellence Model.

The leadership approach was a big change for some organisations that had a management system such as ISO 9001:2008 and had left it, chiefly, to middle management to run after signing off on some high-level policies. In broad terms, the organisations that already had a leadership model for their management systems found transitioning to the 2015 version of ISO 9001 more straightforward.

Annex SL assumes that top management can be the same as leadership or, in some organisations, top management and leadership will be different parties – from an individual or a group to a governance entity. The best example would be in a small-to-medium enterprise (SME), where top management and leadership may be the same person or persons. However, in a bigger organisation the chief executive might be top manager, but other directors will be treated as leaders. The key point is that the management system belongs to the top management and leadership – not just middle managers.

The other potential inhibitor, at a strategic level, to implementing an IMS is the current individual board responsibilities for different types of risk-based management systems. For example, the board member responsible for quality, health and safety and environmental management could be three or more individuals. This could continue with an IMS. They might work as top management (i.e. top management doesn't necessarily mean one individual), or they could be a leadership team under the chief executive as top manager. However, both these approaches require close co-operation between the board members concerned, with a firm plan or protocol in place to ensure that the IMS decision-making process doesn't become siloed again or unduly bureaucratic.

One broader point to remember upfront is that the risk-based thinking requirements of Annex SL should create interest within top management and leadership – deciding upon and managing risk is within their sphere of decision making.

PDCA

PDCA has been the cornerstone of the many assessable ISO standards, long before Annex SL. However, the way PDCA works within an organisation needs to be understood because it can provide an exciting – and very effective – focus to the way the organisation moves towards an IMS. This is why it is worth being reminded how PDCA works as its principles may have been pushed to the back of the virtual filing cabinet over the years.[4]

PDCA is sometimes thought of as only applying to one management system – the ISO standards show how PDCA applies to their particular standard, e.g. ISO 14001:2015. However, an integrated approach applies equally well, if not better, to PDCA.

---

[4] PDCA is sometimes known as the Deming Cycle or Circle after the American quality guru W. Edwards Deming (1900-1993). It is also sometimes known as the Shewhart Cycle after another American, the engineer and statistician Walter A. Shewhart (1891–1967). Today, the Shewhart Cycle typically refers to a statistical process control version of PDCA – hence why Deming Cycle is often seen as a more generic application of the approach.

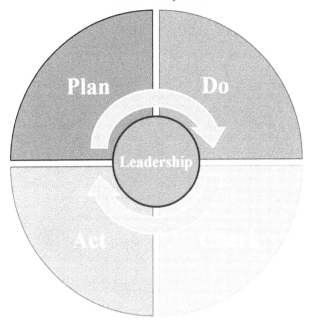

Figure 2: The PDCA cycle

In short, PDCA is a circular approach to management: we **plan**, communicate and then mobilise a process, then we **do** or carry out the process (or processes) including making minor adjustments, and then we **check** if the process has performed as anticipated (this, of course, could be under or overperformance). This is the **check** phase (sometimes called the learning phase or after action review). Once we understand why performance variations occurred, the leadership team can decide a way forward, including deciding how to prevent reoccurrence of the process variation.

Then we **act** (or standardise or calibrate) the process. This is based on the outcome of the **check** phase. This phase forms part of the continual improvement approach and is fed back into the **plan** phase of the cycle. When it is sometimes said that Annex

SL standards are based on continual improvement, this is normally what is meant.

It doesn't mean, however, that continual improvement can't be determined in other ways, because PDCA is an umbrella, not a straitjacket. While PDCA remains the bedrock of all Annex SL standards, it is also useful for an IMS based on other approaches, e.g. the check phase of PDCA aligns well with Six Sigma and Lean approaches; the plan and act phases can be aligned with EFQM-type approaches. PDCA can certainly be aligned with some health and safety approaches, such as the UK Health and Safety Executive's HSG65 management model.

Risk-based thinking

Before Annex SL, the various ISO standards that could be used for a third-party assessment had different requirements and expectations about risk. This is sometimes forgotten and can be an inhibitor to an IMS implementation if it isn't reflected upon at an early stage.

For example, ISO 14001:2004 implied that risk had to be considered within specific requirements (for example, defining environmental aspects and impacts; deciding upon emergency preparedness and response procedures) but there was no requirement to have the whole EMS working on a risk-based thinking model, directed by leadership. ISO 14001:2015, drafted in accordance with Annex SL, completely changed this.

The ISO describes risk-based thinking as;

> inherent in all aspects of a quality management system. There are risks in all systems, processes and functions. Risk-based thinking ensures these risks are identified, considered and controlled throughout the design and use of the quality management system.[5]

---

[5] ISO, *Risk-based thinking in ISO 9001:2015.*

While the example given relates to ISO 9001:2015, it applies to virtually all management system examples. The complicated bit is:

a) That the organisation accepts risk-based thinking as an approach; and

b) What that particular organisation sees as risk and opportunities – within its management system.

There may be considerable variation about what an organisation sees as risks it recognises or wishes to treat. The notion of exploiting opportunities and minimising risk sounds so obvious but often isn't. This can be a challenge when implementing an IMS. One strategic thought is the leadership team.

Where an organisation already has a detailed approach to risk management, aligning this with risk-based thinking may seem simple. An IMS approach normally fits in well with this because risk registers or enterprise risk management (ERM)-type systems often look at the whole organisation and not at risk in silos. Indeed, the headache can be deciding what risks the IMS will influence or control, rather than the wider financial and political risks that these risk register-type systems will often assume. Some practical approaches to defining risk-based thinking within an organisation is discussed later.

However, it is important to bear in mind that, in the context of Annex SL, risks mean uncertainty in meeting agreed objectives (although some individual standards have tweaked this). Also, some standards such as ISO 27001 and ISO 22001, despite having sector-specific approaches to risk, treatment and control, still adhere to the same high-level principles of what risks the organisation wishes to mitigate and the opportunities it wishes to exploit. Remember that thinking in silos isn't just functional – it can be encouraged by standards being interpreted as creating their own special universe that nothing and no one can impact upon. Arguably, until very recently, this is how some leadership teams looked at information security – something they employed other people to think about. However, the IMS highlights that the tactical specifics of risk control in areas like information security and food safety can only help generate ideas and approaches – they are certainly not different approaches to organisational risk. Also, these examples help a leadership team understand that the integrated approach reduces uncertainty.

So, there is an element of chicken and egg. With an IMS, objectives can't be agreed until the organisation's own view of risk is understood; equally, the uncertainties an organisation really wants to avoid will drive deciding on objectives. One simple example is the need to drive down reject rates of a product; there are risks and opportunities (or benefits) with investing in this strategy, but if the issue is ignored then the risk to sales, reputation and rework budgets could be critical. It is for leadership to decide where its focus is going to be, which might be partly driven not just by customers, but other stakeholders' expectations (who are known as interested parties under Annex SL).

Equally, the targets or other outcomes an organisation really wants to achieve can form at least part of the opportunities aspects of objectives, e.g. better than anticipated conversion rates on a new business acquisition. Or an opportunity might be seen as generating a better performance – or better minimisation of risk – than originally planned for. Without monitoring and measuring processes it would be difficult to quantify any changes – hence why Annex SL also requires these processes.

CHAPTER 3: IMS IMPLEMENTATION STRATEGIES

Does an IMS always have to be aligned to any particular management standards?

The short answer is no.

An IMS does not have to align to any particular standard(s) or proprietary specifications or schemes. An organisation could design its own policies and processes and then create an IMS from these.

Standards like ISO 9001 have generated criticism, such as from the management consultant John Seddon,[6] who sees complying with ISO 9001 as leading to sub-optimisation rather than improvement in performance. Critics of ISO standards tend to argue that diversion of resources to meet their requirements and preparing for third-party assessments don't generate the improvements claimed. However, a far wider group of professional opinion would argue otherwise. Who is right? In reality, it all depends on each organisation and its circumstances, including the expectations of their customers. Any organisation whose aim is to implement an IMS needs to conduct a cost-benefit analysis or a similar process to determine whether an IMS is the way for them. There is no golden means on this.

So, there is no requirement to have an IMS that follows any particular ISO standard unless an organisation's customer or other stakeholder demands this. Also, organisations could follow a different standard, proprietary specification or management approach, or any combination of them. These might include the EFQM Excellence Model or, say, Lean or Six Sigma. These very different approaches could individually, or even collectively, provide a focal point to implementing an IMS.

---

[6] John Seddon, *The Case Against ISO9000: How to Create Real Quality in Your Organisation*, Oak Tree Press, 2000.

Indeed, there are a number of safety and IT security specifications or schemes that could be adapted to wider IMS requirements. Looking at these from a wider risk content than they were originally designed for can, for some organisations, be an effective starting point to determine what their attitude to risk is and how they wish to respond to it in terms of processes and systems. The aim is to mitigate and treat risk, not just to integrate processes and procedures for the sake of it.

For those who are not familiar with EFQM, see:

www.efqm.org

For Six Sigma and Lean, the American Society for Quality has a page that explains these concepts:

https://asq.org/quality-resources/six-sigma

However, the range of standards, specifications and so forth integrated within an organisation can create their own complexity. Never lose sight of what is trying to be achieved by integration and collecting (or endorsing) a whole range of badges that may not necessarily be the best use of resources.

One key reason why many an IMS will follow two or more ISO standards is the fact that many organisations have contractual or other reasons for adopting such standards, whether any or all of these are formally assessed by a third-party CB or not.

Also, what management processes are included within an IMS is up to the organisation, i.e. there may still be some areas of risk treated separately, e.g. information security and business continuity management may sometimes fall within this approach as they are sometimes seen as using different sets of risk treatment tools (although there is no reason why they shouldn't be included within an IMS and sometimes are).

The decision to base any IMS upon any standard, specification or scheme is an early and critical one. For one thing, the nature of the IMS will be influenced by those products and, indeed, where an organisation has both ISO 9001 and Six Sigma will often create a number of challenges to align the requirements and expectations. To add something like environmental management or health and safety into the mix leads to a degree of strategic and creative thinking to ensure policy and objectives can effectively sit above the different strands of tactical and systems-based delivery.

To this end, the next chapter will look at some of the principles that can influence decision making on IMS design. The examples discussed are based on the leadership, risk-based and process approaches of ISO standards. However, they could have been taken from, say, the EFQM Excellence Model or other approaches.

The key point is that any approach simply provides a bridge between strategy and tactics in implementing an IMS. Being too precious about whether the exact requirements of any approach are being met should be avoided, especially in the early stages of implementation. Crossing 'i's and dotting 't's is for a later time in the IMS implementation.

Strategic buy-in

As outlined in the previous chapter, there are a number of concepts or guidelines that could help plan an IMS implementation. Just as importantly, they will help define what the IMS policy and objectives can achieve. While we are looking at the topics discussed in chapter two, the intention is to create a forum of discussion points to ensure that any leadership team can clearly understand what it can achieve from an IMS as well as what its initial or preconceived impressions may be.

How far does Annex SL help a leadership team with thinking about an IMS?

As we've already seen, the Annex SL HLS does what it says on the tin. It means that all future assessable ISO standards will need to follow the high-level requirements outlined in Annex SL.

Look again at our quote from ISO:

> Annex SL harmonizes structure, text and terms and definitions, while leaving the standards developers with the flexibility to integrate their specific technical topics and requirements.[7]

If we swap "standards developers" for "leadership", this sounds more like an IMS – at least from a systems approach.

Each organisation will have its own risk appetite – the extent to which it is comfortable in accepting levels of residual or even higher levels of risk. Risk appetite in a big organisation is not necessarily constant, e.g. risk taking may be encouraged in some entrepreneurial activities, but risk is not accepted in any way relating to, say, safety. The approach taken by any board isn't just down to personalities, but the dictates of owners, regulators, major customers and other stakeholders. But aligning these discussions with the advantages of an IMS should be the key focus.

As previously stated, Annex SL assumes that all management systems should be leadership led and managed and, finally, that risk-based thinking is used throughout the PDCA model. This means some organisations that already adopt these standards have already devised these risk-based policies and objectives. They may simply need some common themes drawn from them to move towards IMS requirements.

For example, an organisation with ISO 27001:2013 and ISO 22301:2012 will now be working to a common HLS, even though both these standards have their own specific requirements.

Why should leadership be interested in an IMS?

We know that Annex SL requires management systems to be leadership led, but this has not always been the case with ISO

---

[7] *www.iso.org/news/2012/07/Ref1621.html.*

standards. The leadership approach was a big change for some organisations that had a management system such as ISO 9001:2008, which could have been left, chiefly, to middle management. By ensuring risks and objectives are led by senior management, whose decisions will take into account all aspects of an organisation, an organisation develops an integrated approach to their management.

The decision-making structure that will champion the IMS needs to be clear before a leadership-led discussion on uncertainty can be had. This sounds obvious but needs to be clarified before the next stage, discussed below, can begin.

PDCA and managing uncertainty

We discussed PDCA in the previous chapter. Some leadership teams see it almost as the territory of wonks – or boffins for older readers! This is not the case. Again, when setting policies and objectives, understanding how processes contribute to continual improvement can only help clarify what an IMS will mean to each organisation, and how processes and procedures can sometimes be better designed and delivered in an integrated way.

Before considering PDCA, the organisation's strategic direction should be understood. There are various ways this could be quantified or calibrated depending on the size of the organisation. For example, a Strengths, Weaknesses, Opportunities and Threats (SWOT) analysis might be appropriate. Or, to put it another way, PDCA assumes we have some idea of the destination we are aiming for, even if this changes as the circular process model of continual improvement rolls forward.

One other key point should be kept in mind – PDCA doesn't necessarily imply a risk-based management system. For example, ISO 9001:2008 was PDCA based but didn't require risk-based thinking. In essence, PDCA isn't necessarily anything to do with risk-based thinking, but Annex SL has aligned the concepts together in a way that supports both approaches. So, although many were already using the approach before it became an Annex SL requirement, never assume an organisation will understand a risk-based PDCA. It is also worth considering that an IMS can assist bringing risk-based thinking into an organisation, as the integrated approach will usually bring together strategic thinking about risks and opportunities in a way that a siloed approach to management may not.

In essence, PDCA is not an inhibitor to setting up an IMS because the approach originally devised for quality management can be adapted to almost any process-based requirement, be it safety, environmental management or information security to name a few. This is because PDCA is an umbrella below which a whole raft of supporting processes and concepts can sit.

If the process is broken down into PDCA stages, each stage shows what is required of the process – rather than what each functional area is responsible for. PDCA can be interpreted just for quality, or just for information security, but arguably that isn't PDCA because we are applying artificial ringfences around – especially – the check and act stages. This creates unnecessary risks of matters falling between the cracks.

So, one helpful way of using PDCA when discussing an IMS implementation is to use its individual stages against specific processes. For example, resource management (be this human or infrastructure resources) can lend itself well to showing how each element of PDCA helps integrated ways of working. This is often true where approaches to, say, safety or adherence to password policies can be broken down into elements from employment interviews, staff appraisals, identified competency needs, training and ongoing supervision.

At worst, these can be 'gatekeeper' approaches to staff management that leadership rarely involves itself in, unless it is a very senior hire. But PDCA can be used to demonstrate how a more enhanced approach to safety and IT security could be achieved for little additional effort, i.e. why would an organisation employ someone new at, say, middle-management level if they didn't display any understanding or desire to follow safety or IT security policies? The same might apply to ethical, anti-bribery and corporate responsibility goals.

While different middle managers may be responsible for recruitment, safety, IT security and anti-bribery, a PDCA could change this to an integrated management approach. Instead of various managers approaching the recruiting process differently, an integrated system would ensure that there was a universal recruitment process. This would minimise risks and maximise opportunities when new employees enter the organisation. In simplistic terms, this might be ensuring all interviewees are asked questions about all these risk and value points and their answers recorded. It also means the interviewers need to explain something about the organisation's values and policies to the candidate. This integrated approach minimises the risk of employing those whose values are different to those of the organisation.

The example above is just one scenario where a leadership approach can drill straight down into operational process. In the example given, no middle-management responsibilities change – simply the recruitment process takes into account all the integrated requirements of only employing those in managerial roles who understand and support the organisation's values and risk profile. This is risk-based thinking in action. In fact, an IMS can be designed to support good internal communication; arguably, a risk control and potentially an opportunity too.

Of course, it might mean those middle managers responsible for recruitment, safety and so forth might talk to one another more about the risk and opportunities they manage as they have an involvement in the process. A good thing, surely, and something leadership may see as a benefit.

IMS and process-based thinking

Many fine words could be written about the difference between process-based approaches to management compared with others, e.g. procedural-based approaches. In some small organisations a procedural-based approach is attractive. I have seen a number of SMEs where a procedural-based approach – based on ISO 9001:1994 (long defunct!) – is still the underlying basis of their QMS; the same might be said for some health and safety systems in lower-risk SME operations.

The difference between process and procedural approaches can be a useful starting point when an organisation asks itself if integrating management systems will be beneficial. This is especially so if some parts of the organisation use procedures and other parts rely on different process-type guidance. Equally, different parts of the process can have differing levels of maturity, and an IMS implementation will tend to highlight these; or to put it another way, an IMS can be an effective driver towards consistency both in terms of process maturity as well as consistency of product or service delivery.

One useful overarching concept to keep in mind is that of continual improvement within PDCA, i.e. improvement flows from lessons learned after we have measured our performance – those lessons learned are then built into the plan element of PDCA. While this may have originally been a QMS concept, it can apply to any management system and certainly applies to any IMS implementation. If a leadership team is asked to discuss what it sees as its continual improvement achievements in recent months and then considers how far these have been down to better process control and procedural understanding – or lack of it – then these can help formulate ideas about how a more integrated approach to process delivery will be powerful.

IMS, risk and metrics

Before Annex SL, ISO standards had different requirements and expectations about risk. For example, ISO 14001:2004 implied that risk had to be considered within specific requirements (for example, defining environmental aspects and impacts; deciding upon emergency preparedness and response procedures) but there was no requirement to have the whole EMS working on a risk-based thinking model, directed by leadership. ISO 14001:2015, drafted in accordance with Annex SL, completely changed this. Remember, in the context of Annex SL, risks mean uncertainty in meeting agreed objectives (although some individual standards have tweaked this).

Risk and objectives need to relate to what the management systems can directly influence, e.g. purely financial or political risks aren't directly influenced or controlled by an IMS. Where an organisation just wants to focus on these types of risk, it suggests that the organisation may not fully understand what its current QMS, EMS or even ISMS does for it in terms of managing risk! A shortfall in understanding can be turned into continual improvement just with that simple realisation.

How does this risk-based thinking impact on policy and objectives?

The notion of exploiting opportunities and minimising risk sounds so obvious but often isn't so easy to see in practice. The consequences and likelihood of failure, coupled with the challenges and resources involved with achieving even moderate success, are all big factors when any senior manager makes that express or implied calculation in their mind as to whether to proceed with a business decision or not. Such a mindset can be a challenge when implementing an IMS until, there is a level of understanding that an IMS can reduce the risk curve considerably if an integrated approach to management systems is taken.

But how can these decisions be made? What evidence supports them? One way of reaching integrated objectives using risk-based thinking is to look at the metrics currently used.

In some approaches to management systems, such as Six Sigma, the monitoring and measuring processes that exist to show the level of conformity achieved and consistency of process outputs are fundamental. There is no way of escaping measurement and then the analysis of it. With ISO standards this is also true, but not to the same extent unless the management system is implemented based on these similar hard metrics – perhaps using some statistical process control, i.e. the Deming Cycle has become a Shewhart Cycle. And there will be many management systems where some metrics are softer, i.e. achieving policy deliverables, redesigning processes, conducting more detailed stakeholder reviews and so forth, which can only be measured by the way they will eventually generate more measurable outputs, e.g. increased sales, increased compliance with IT security protocols, fewer near misses, better recycling rates.

However, I have seen many instances where assumptions are made as to the accuracy of all figures presented to a leadership team. There might be simple arithmetic errors. The sample size may not be as big as the report implies. Some products or processes might have been excluded from the sample (either in error or by design). Some near misses were simply not recorded or the records not consolidated, so statistics could not be pulled from them. Relatively minor data breaches may have been unreported or, again, not compiled, so any emerging risk patterns couldn't be accurately discerned. Yet some leadership teams only look at the outputs and may not question what might have escaped the net. They could be making risk-based decisions without all the key information to make them in the most effective way.

Or, of course, as we've already mentioned, some Six Sigma and Lean approaches only look at certain aspects of process conformity and not others, e.g. we keep achieving higher scores – shame about safety and IT security not following suit! This is an issue with the organisation – not Six Sigma. Risk-based thinking can be used to concentrate minds on why such events have evolved and how metrics can resolve them.

An integrated approach should go back to the basics of what all these different reports are setting out to achieve and how consistent the process of generating reports is. Some may use the various 'dashboard' tools on the market or couple them with other approaches. The important point is that integration may simply mean all the different strands of reporting are considered as a whole. This doesn't necessarily mean whole new sets of metrics are put into place. That may be an outcome, but it is a mistake to assume that will always be the case with an IMS.

The other risk in monitoring and measuring processes of different management systems, is the risk of duplication by treating each process in its own way. For example, the monitoring of call handling times in a call centre might ignore whether data protection protocols are followed – very easy to forget as an agent if you are under pressure to deal with so many calls per hour. So, an organisation could have one director who is ensuring that employees' customer service targets are being achieved however, a different director will be evaluating whether the call centre staff are following data protection protocols. Instead of working in silos, an organisation could establish an IMS and this would enable a universal management system. This would prevent the call centre staff being managed by two different directors, and would highlight that meeting customer service targets should take into consideration the time it takes for data protection protocols to be followed. This is where an IMS can be powerful – not only do we avoid duplication but we also understand the risk universe much better, and that meeting a customer target is more complex than it can appear.

Another example – which we will come back to later – is a warehouse where chemicals are being stored for a customer. So, we have quality-related measures e.g. are we only using approved suppliers to source the chemicals? The health and safety measures might include reporting on how we are complying with storing these chemicals according to company procedures. The environmental manager will be looking at how we are storing them in a way that minimises the risk of accidental and sudden pollution, thereby reducing the potential of an environmental incident. There will be all manner of records and inspections going on, often by separate supervisors or managers, often with their own metrics and particular priorities. Is there any advantage to such duplication? An IMS would ensure that the monitoring and measurement looks at broader issues, i.e. is the pollution risk greater than the safety risk due to the way the chemicals need to be stored? In other words, are we checking and re-checking things that present a lesser risk than some other matters, yet it is still done because it is that supervisor's responsibility to check on this or that every day, irrespective of importance?

Or to put it another way, operating in silos can also apply to reporting. A higher risk than inaccurate reporting is leadership not seeing the interrelationship between risk-based reporting. For example, an increase in comparatively minor data breaches might suggest evolving shortfalls in recruitment or line management supervision processes. There are many other possible scenarios where evidence from one technical or functional area isn't linked with that from another. Indeed, those familiar with the 'Swiss cheese' risk model[8] will know the idea of how an unplanned event (be it an accident, data breach or process nonconformity) can arise even if there are many layers of defence in between. Siloed reporting and review can create such a risk or rather, hide any potential alignment of events that prevent controls being effective. This is one reason why a management review process is so important in an IMS as well as in ISO standards. The monitoring and measurement processes that report into that meeting(s) enable a forum to review all the risk data against current risk assumptions across the whole organisation, and not just in IT security or quality concern.

Integration applies to leadership thinking – it is their risk-based thinking – just as much as integrating day-to-day process controls.

All of these steps assume policy and objectives have been agreed for the IMS. We will now consider how this might be approached as the implementation of the IMS will flow directly from the decisions made about policy and objectives.

---

[8] *www.ncbi.nlm.nih.gov/pmc/articles/PMC1117770/*.

CHAPTER 4: IMPLEMENTING AN IMS – POLICIES AND OBJECTIVES

Top management and leadership need to have a clear vision of the IMS and its timescales for implementation.

They also need to appreciate the initial cost of resourcing the change management. An IMS might well lead to efficiencies in all respects, but these will not be achieved without at least some resources being deployed.

Indeed, one way to approach whether an IMS is the way to go is to complete a gap analysis. This will determine how far the journey will be to achieve an IMS and therefore, the likely resources needed. Opportunity cost can play a part here in decision making unless new resources are injected to make the transition to an IMS a reality.

As we have already touched on, unless the organisation is very large and complex, the aim should be to have one board member responsible to the chief executive for the IMS on a day-to-day basis. In any event, there needs to be at least an element of support from the whole board – it needs to enable the IMS. Personalities, professional responsibilities and egos can all come into play in reaching such an agreement. It may seem tempting to put the cart before the horse, but don't.

The leadership team (including the board) shouldn't begin to set policy and objectives for an IMS until it has decided how their roles and responsibilities will also change.

Policy

If an organisation already has an Annex SL-based standard in place, it will be familiar with the notion of setting a policy that objectives sit under. In practical terms, the policy is the highest statement of the management system, to which objectives and operational processes and controls sit below. It is not just a visionary statement or, dare I say, a lot of nice-sounding guff to try to impress stakeholders or potential customers.

Phrases are sometimes found in policy statements like "zero harm", "zero waste to landfill", "total reliability" and "100% customer satisfaction" among others. However sincerely these statements may be meant, they don't really mean anything specific. That is, until they are qualified and quantified with specific objectives to measure performance and the processes needed to achieve the desired outcomes. In practical terms, an organisation should be able to devise its own internal IMS audit plans from the policy statement for the whole management system – if it can't then the policy statement may be too broad and visionary.

Also, the management systems' objectives should be derived from the policy and certainly not conflict with it. I have seen a number of objectives that bear no relationship to the policy statement and even less relationship to the day-to-day processes and procedures delivering the core product or service. And whether Annex SL principles are being followed or not, it makes little – if any – sense to do this within a management systems arena. Indeed, with an IMS, these expectations of the policy can assist the implementation process itself.

If the IMS is going to follow Annex SL requirements, separate policy statements that previously supported, say, ISO 9001 and ISO 14001 become one IMS policy. This could be an entirely new statement – doing this might help some boards in discussing why they are starting the IMS journey and what tangible benefits they are looking to reap from it. The other approach would be a merger of the current management system's separate policy statements. The aim is to avoid a rehash. Instead, use the review process to see where the policy statements have commonalities and where the organisation has moved on to different expectations.

Where some management systems are not being included within an IMS, e.g. where ISO 9001 and ISO 14001 are being integrated but ISO 27001 – the ISMS – is being left standalone, some areas of commonality may arise, such as customer expectations for secure transmission of their data while in the organisation's care. An IMS can influence other areas of business systems not currently in its orbit. At the very least, examining this question of any commonality between different policy statements can contribute to understanding what an IMS can now achieve – and might achieve later – for an organisation.

Looking at all these points starts a discussion and from that an IMS policy will follow. It may be a straightforward decision, or it may take longer for agreement to be reached. Sometimes a provisional policy statement might be agreed and then calibrated after objectives are determined.

However, it is essential that something is agreed before objectives are set. Remember, the policy does have a true purpose – it is not just fine words or traders' puff – it acts as a shop window into the IMS.

Objectives

With an Annex SL system, the objectives are effectively the choices that leadership has – currently – made as to the risk and opportunities it wishes the management system to focus upon. Objectives are not set in stone and can be amended or calibrated based on changes to the organisational environment or measurement outcomes. Those organisations that follow Six Sigma or Lean-type approaches will understand this straight away; objectives will evolve based on results.

One common inhibitor to setting objectives is the concern that they might become inflexible. This is simply not true. Top management (in conjunction with stakeholders) can be flexible and change objectives at any time. It can show an organisation is flexible if it can review its objectives regularly, rather than just re-ratifying them annually. In fact, if PDCA is being followed, it is almost inevitable that objectives will need to be calibrated, if not significantly changed, based on operational experience. This process of calibration or updating is part of a continual improvement process.

Where an IMS is being created from existing management systems, there is one important strategic decision to be made at the outset: are completely new objectives going to be set, or are the desired outcomes going to be culled from the existing objectives for the constituent management system? Again, a talking point for the leadership team, and some members may not have looked at the objectives closely during that time.

With Annex SL systems (and with Lean, Six Sigma and EFQM), there is some expectation that the objectives will be measurable. Before deciding on objectives, consider what metrics will be required, what is already in place and what resources can be found to improve existing measurement processes. There is little point in defining any objectives that aren't measurable, or where metrics are going to be difficult or onerous to achieve consistently. Some organisations may be tempted to define objectives first and not consider measurement until later. This is almost certainly a mistake. While there are many definitions of risk, if we accept that it is the things that keep the leadership team awake at night, so to speak, then measuring how effectively we are managing and trying to minimise these risks is critical.

While there is much spoken about the known unknowns and even the unknown unknowns, the greater practical issue for many organisations is being aware of both the key risks and opportunities in the first place and, in turn, having accurate, ongoing data about exposure. In other words, we might be applying too many controls to one risk and not enough to another, yet over a period, more effective performance data would have suggested the decision should be the other way around; concepts like accident aetiology and emerging risks come to mind. This is often true in areas such as information security or health and safety, where the risk universe is so great a leadership team must decide where best to put its risk control and treatment resources. Leaders can only make risk-based decisions based on best information to hand. So, without measurable objectives – and monitoring and measurements systems to support them – this is virtually impossible to achieve.

While this could all sound more like inhibitors than enablers, it means the decision to do something about risk leads to quite the reverse. Certainly, with Annex SL systems, the working assumption is always that the management system – the day-to-day operational controls – is there to support the objectives, i.e. to minimise risk and maximise any opportunities. It is not just a set of processes and procedures to be followed because the management system says so. Once there is strategic understanding of this point, setting objectives should become a clearer and often more dynamic process, i.e. instead of scratching our heads as to what we might call a risk-based objective, the risks that could be included will present themselves in a more obvious way.

What should the objectives say?

Initially, the organisation should avoid setting many objectives as they will all take resources to measure and monitor. What constitutes 'many' depends on the circumstances. I once saw a multinational project management business that had created an IMS out of six individual Annex SL standards. The type and number of objectives it had to set would be different to, say, a project management business of 50 people where two Annex SL standards were being integrated together.

With Annex SL standards there is no expectation that all metrics will be hard – it all depends on stakeholder expectations and the core business requirements. For example, an objective to introduce an enhanced staff appraisal process could be hard in the sense that we can keep figures on how many staff have had the enhanced processed delivered to them. However, whether the enhanced performance that was planned for did indeed improve competency or increase safe behaviours or whatever the goals were will often come down to leadership judgement later.

When collecting hard metric data, the organisation needs to understand the importance of accuracy i.e. what checks and controls are in place to make sure accurate figures are presented on performance? So, when deciding upon objectives, early questions should always be:

- How complex will it be to produce accurate data?
- What limitations may the sampling have, if any?

This is important because inconsistent or incomplete data doesn't prove anything but will provide a false sense of security about risk. Alternatively – and almost as unwelcome – is that it could lead to a lot more risk treatments being undertaken than actually necessary.

Rather like the example above, some objectives will lean towards an integrated approach – all aspects of a management system could be enhanced through better staff appraisal and better understanding of competency. There may be specific objectives relating to one management system, e.g. setting a target to reduce near misses is very specific towards ISO 45001. Yet the objective might be achieved, in part, by improved work instructions (ISO 9001) and more realistic delivery targets agreed with clients (ISO 9001).

So, the objective itself might be specific but the metrics will be more integrated. This is often true with non-human resources, e.g. infrastructure and the work environment, which meets environmental, health and safety, and information security quality requirements – defining risk-based objectives that recognise all these expectations is all that is required.

Communication with top management and the rest of the leadership team is the reoccurring theme when discussing policy and objectives. Of course, different layers of management, consultants and even other stakeholders (such as owners or other controlling entities) might have a role in advising the leadership team. But where a leadership team decides to leave policy and objective setting to middle management – and then merely signs it off – it can certainly be an inhibitor to a productive implementation of an IMS. Everyone has a role in implementing an IMS, including the organisation's leadership team.

CHAPTER 5: ACTING ON THE IMS

Mind the gap

Once policy and objectives have been agreed, the next part of the IMS implementation process is to consider how far the management system has been integrated already. This may be quite irrespective of what the management system may say to the contrary. While this might be expected with management systems that have been combined to a greater or lesser extent, it might be found even where this hasn't formally begun.

Interestingly, process staff (and especially their supervisory management) may not always be fully aware of how far they have integrated these processes; this is something to bear in mind when reviewing what needs to be done within an IMS implementation. Always look at the written or diagrammatic expression of the process as well as listening to what staff say they do. There may sometimes be differences or, at least, assume boundaries have been crossed.

For example, if separate health and safety and environmental manuals have been operating, this doesn't mean that some processes haven't evolved into more integrated steps, e.g. the safe use of spill kits may have already been included within toolbox talks, as well as how to deploy them to minimise the impact of pollution incidents. Equally, a quality manual may often implement parts of an environmental manual as well as the health and safety manual, e.g. just-in-time ordering of chemicals will minimise the need for storing these potentially toxic substances, which in turn will help minimise safety and pollution risks. There can be similar links between the quality and information security manual, e.g. how GDPR requirements are controlled within the day-to-day operational processes for information security will also meet customer expectations as well.

The examples above are just a handful among many potential areas that might be found. They are likely to have arisen because the process has evolved in an integrated way, just for practical reasons, but the manuals were written independently and at different times. They may also have been audited completely separately and reported to leadership separately in terms of any findings, i.e. fully siloed.

Taking one of the above examples, the quality auditor had been interested in whether the just-in-time ordering process was being followed consistently; the environmental auditor had been interested in whether anti-pollution controls were still in place; and the safety auditor was interested in whether the COSHH Regulations were always understood and being applied.

Usually this type of siloed auditing can occur with the very best intentions. One comparatively straightforward approach to beginning an IMS implementation is to review not only the documented management systems that form part of the integration, but also the internal audit reports and any external assessment reports. Patterns of commonality can often be identified by the comments of auditors and assessors. They can give useful indications of where some level of integration has already been achieved.

Unless an organisation has a very flat structure, there will always be a functional element to it, and some managers only focus on what they are directly told to report about. An IMS implementation can help an organisation move towards a more opportunities based approach to management, i.e. a holistic approach to how customer and other stakeholder requirements are met. This is more than fine words as it is critically looking at how processes interact and how this makes people think about their contribution to the organisation, and how others also contribute to it – be this the chief executive or the most junior member of staff.

All these factors explain why objectives can need some minor amendments during the early stages of IMS implementation – any commonalities identified can lead to better risk controls being in place than anticipated, or opportunities that were not quantified. Alternatively, processes or procedures that the leadership see as important might not be in place any longer.

The touchstone is this: does the process support the objectives? If the answer is 'no' or 'not sure', then more investigation or reflection is needed.

Where Six Sigma, Lean or other process control systems are in place instead of Annex SL approaches, it is important that the metrics are agreed for the areas of integration before leadership reviews are restructured. These efficiency (or more explicitly waste reduction) methodologies may need to extend to other areas, e.g. health and safety. However, they may have already been included, i.e. some organisations prefer to see actions less than optimally safe as being inefficient or waste. Of course, if terms like inefficiency or waste reduction need to have clearer definitions – or boundaries for the organisation itself – this can be done as a part of the IMS strategy. Often different disciplines may have taken slightly different approaches and this needs to be identified as soon as possible.

Where all these circumstances present themselves to an organisation, a gap analysis may be desirable – the gap analysis report findings then highlight any issues that need to be addressed at both strategic and more tactical levels.

Pursuing the project

Once the current integrated status of the management systems is understood, the implementation can continue.

An implementation plan is now essential. Some organisations might see it as a project with milestones defined. The more complex the implementation, the more formal the project plan. If the IMS implementation is not treated as a project, there could be open-ended timescales involved. The milestones and any other deadlines should be based on the way the IMS is going to be rolled out.

A top-down approach is often appropriate. By this it is meant that the integration has already begun at high level, e.g. policy, objectives and leadership involvement have been achieved.

The way internal IMS auditing will evolve is already being highlighted – one thing that should be explained during implementation is that an IMS often leads to less auditing. However, the less audit fatigue message needs to be tempered with the fact that the audits may be more detailed.

While it is one approach, trying to incorporate or cross-reference siloed procedures may not be the best idea.

Remember, ISO standards tend to treat process consistency as the holy grail, whereas Six Sigma or Lean would see the same holy grail as efficiency or waste minimisation, so the desired outcome will have impacted on the way processes were designed. In some respects, an IMS might straddle both the holy grails depending on the process element or stakeholder being satisfied.

In some organisations, there will be potential inhibitors through the influence of professional disciplines, e.g. HR, IT management, finance, procurement, safety professionals and engineers among others. Rather than fighting against disciplines, embrace them. In other words, unless the process or procedure is so complex that it cannot be understood by other professionals, it should not be an inhibitor. Even where it is, this is where the discipline professional, e.g. the HR manager, can be involved in ensuring the documented system becomes more integrated with say, health and safety and environmental matters and not just the quality slant it currently has.

Staff engagement is vital. Some organisations will have consultation processes already in place for other purposes. One aim would be to look at processes and procedure at operator level – be this team administrator, warehouse picking, junior engineer or whoever is 'at the coalface'.

At each stage of the process there needs to be an agreed approach for a leadership representative to review each stage of the implementation, i.e. milestones shouldn't just come and go. Also, some further gap analysis audits could be considered as the project progresses, i.e. are milestones being met or is that just written processes and procedures being changed?

Equally, all levels of staff within the organisation need to be consulted – this might be a committee, or it might be more informal groups in different parts of the organisation. The project should emphasise that the IMS belongs to everyone and it is there to reduce bureaucracy and improve processes.

In one sense, the implementation won't stop by a particular date. The 'completion' might be when the updated documented management system is considered implemented or where it could be audited by a third party. However, the project plan should allow for further reviews for an agreed period of time after completion. If the organisation is dynamic, the implementation will continue evolving.

Conclusion

Implementing an IMS can bring many advantages, not just in terms of reducing process duplication and bureaucracy, but in managing risk and providing more focused leadership involvement.

The last chapter explains the process of third-party assessment for organisations that want to consider this approach. However, getting a badge isn't the ideal goal to achieve an IMS – instead it should be about maximising opportunity while minimising risk.

CHAPTER 6: THIRD-PARTY ASSESSMENT

Is it worth considering?

If an organisation already has, say, ISO 9001 and ISO 14001, the process of external assessment to complete an IMS is comparatively straightforward: they will approach their CB to schedule an assessment. However, if an organisation is starting from scratch, the decision is more complex.

The key determinant with any assessment product is to decide why you want it. Some organisations believe that without external assessment they would not progress with continual improvement to the same degree. The other extreme would be to decide that you want a certificate simply to prove compliance with a number of standards.

Whatever the reason, drifting into assessment is not worth considering because there are the even greater ongoing commitments of time and resources to maintain it. It is not like passing a driving test. There will always be regular assessments (sometimes called surveillance or continuing assessment). The end of the world is never nigh in certification (although an organisation can sometimes have their certificate removed by their CB and, indeed, they can surrender it themselves, or change their CB).

While it is possible to have assessment to PAS 99, many organisations that need to show their key customers or other stakeholders that they maintain, say, ISO 9001 or ISO 27001, will still need to maintain the separate approvals for these. Some CBs – if they assess the organisation already for two or more standards – can issue a certificate saying the organisation is now operating an IMS to these standards (after successful assessment). All this means is that the organisation has moved from managing its existing management systems separately or combined to an integrated approach. However, of course an organisation does need to show it has achieved this. A reputable CB will never rubber stamp such a significant change.

An organisation should beware of consultants or assessment bodies persuading it to have any external assessments, unless it understands the pros and cons.

The assessment processes

There are a number of CBs that offer IMS assessments. The best approach for an organisation is to verify whether its CB of choice offers IMS products. In the UK, the CB should also be regulated by the United Kingdom Accreditation Service (UKAS). There are non-regulated CBs, but their certificates may not be recognised by all of an organisation's customers or other stakeholders.

CBs can have different processes for existing clients and new ones for IMS assessment. Also, how they assess the adequacy of an existing combined management system, assessed by them, to an IMS stage may differ slightly. So, the choice of CB should not be based on cost, but how its requirements and processes fit into the organisation's expectations.

The CB should be pleased to explain the assessment process in detail and the fees involved. Although it will not be able to give consultancy, it could recommend consultants or provide quotations for training.

If fees and expenses are an important part of the decision, the CB should confirm total cost. All quote day rates (a fee for each assessor day), but there may be other costs, such as application fees. Some CBs charge annual management fees, some charge for issuing certificates, and some charge the assessor's travelling expenses and other disbursements. The CB can also estimate all these costs for the first three years, at the quotation stage.

The other service the CB can provide – before a formal IMS assessment – is a gap analysis. This is where an IMS lead assessor will assess the documented IMS and then give a written opinion on whether your organisation is ready for the initial assessment process itself. This can be provided where an organisation already has a certificate for, say, ISO 9001 or more than one standard.

The gap analysis usually takes one or two days but, of course, larger organisations could pay for a longer period. Even a one-day gap analysis will give very useful information about whether you are on the right track with an IMS in terms of meeting external assessment requirements.

The next step is the assessment itself (sometimes called an extension to scope or change to approval – the CB will confirm). The duration of the assessment is based on headcount, the number of locations under the proposed IMS certification, and risk factors such as the location of the business and the business streams themselves. Although there may be some variation in the number of days all UKAS-approved CBs should quote, these should all be about the same duration. They are regulated businesses with reputations to maintain and income streams to protect.

An organisation should remember that the most important cost is the management time and opportunity cost within its management team, so the assessment fees are only one element of the budget.

A lead assessor will be appointed by the CB, who will contact the organisation – or its consultant – in advance of the assessment to agree an assessment plan. At the end of each assessment a report with a recommendation will be presented.

An assessment is not an exam with a pass mark. All the requirements of an IMS must be met, although there may be different levels of maturity for different elements of the system.

The assessment will be a combination of interviews and looking at documentary evidence (both electronic and hard copy). These must be available at the assessment. All the CBs have a confidentiality agreement process and there should be no need to keep any matters from the lead assessor – if there is an issue about this, it needs to be agreed in advance with the CB. It is certainly not a topic for the assessment opening meeting.

The lead assessor is not a client or a prospect – the organisation's staff should be candid with them. They are trained to believe what the auditee tells them, until it is tested elsewhere in the organisation, so prevarication or obfuscation isn't to be clever commercial negotiation – it can be disastrous for the outcome of an assessment.

Being either adversarial or fawning towards a lead assessor is also counter-productive. A friendly, professional relationship is ideal. If your organisation really feels that it can't work with the lead assessor assigned, this should be discussed with the CB immediately. Suffering in silence tends to lead to problems later in the assessment process that can be difficult to resolve.

The endgame?

The CB might recommend an IMS certificate at the end of the assessment process, or it may require a further assessment to take place. The assessment recommendation is typically based on the type and number of nonconformities raised. The nonconformities are against the process and the organisation – not against individual directors or other members of staff. It should also be remembered that a further assessment doesn't mean your organisation is suboptimal – it simply means that the assessment criteria hasn't yet been fully achieved.

Once the IMS certificate is issued, a programme of continuing assessments or surveillance visits is agreed. Nonconformities can be raised at these visits, and every three years a reassessment takes place.

The endgame isn't really getting the certificate but maintaining it. Yet that needn't be an imposition. It is an opportunity to develop the system. The organisation can use its CB as a sounding board and a resource for future plans and challenges – while it can't act as a consultant, it can provide added value as part of the standard assessment cost.

FURTHER READING

IT Governance Publishing (ITGP) is the world's leading publisher for governance and compliance. Our industry-leading pocket guides, books, training resources and toolkits are written by real-world practitioners and thought leaders. They are used globally by audiences of all levels, from students to C-suite executives.

Our high-quality publications cover all IT governance, risk and compliance frameworks and are available in a range of formats. This ensures our customers can access the information they need in the way they need it.

Other resources you may find useful include:

- *ISO 27001 ISMS Documentation Toolkit Bolt-on*
  www.itgovernancepublishing.co.uk/product/iso-27001-isms-documentation-toolkit-bolt-on
- *ISO 9001 2015 QMS Documentation Toolkit Bolt-on*
  www.itgovernancepublishing.co.uk/product/iso-9001-2015-qms-documentation-toolkit-bolt-on
- *A Guide to Effective Internal Management System Audits – Implementing internal audits as a risk management tool* by Andrew W Nichols
  www.itgovernancepublishing.co.uk/product/a-guide-to-effective-internal-management-system-audits

For more information on ITGP and branded publishing services, and to view our full list of publications, visit *www.itgovernancepublishing.co.uk*.

To receive regular updates from ITGP, including information on new publications in your area(s) of interest, sign up for our newsletter at *www.itgovernancepublishing.co.uk/topic/newsletter*.

Branded publishing

Through our branded publishing service, you can customise ITGP publications with your company's branding.

Find out more at *www.itgovernancepublishing.co.uk/topic/branded-publishing-services*.

Related services

ITGP is part of GRC International Group, which offers a comprehensive range of complementary products and services to help organisations meet their objectives.

For a full range of resources on IMS implementation visit *www.itgovernance.co.uk/management-system-integration*.

Training services

The IT Governance training programme is built on our extensive practical experience designing and implementing management systems based on ISO standards, best practice and regulations.

Our courses help attendees develop practical skills and comply with contractual and regulatory requirements. They also support career development via recognised qualifications.

Learn more about our training courses and view the full course catalogue at *www.itgovernance.co.uk/training*.

Professional services and consultancy

We are a leading global consultancy of IT governance, risk management and compliance solutions. We advise businesses around the world on their most critical issues and present cost-saving and risk-reducing solutions based on international best practice and frameworks.

We offer a wide range of delivery methods to suit all budgets, timescales and preferred project approaches.

Further reading

Find out how our consultancy services can help your organisation at *www.itgovernance.co.uk/consulting*.

Industry news

Want to stay up to date with the latest developments and resources in the IT governance and compliance market? Subscribe to our Daily Sentinel newsletter and we will send you mobile-friendly emails with fresh news and features about your preferred areas of interest, as well as unmissable offers and free resources to help you successfully start your projects. *www.itgovernance.co.uk/daily-sentinel*.

EU for product safety is Stephen Evans, The Mill Enterprise Hub, Stagreenan, Drogheda, Co. Louth, A92 CD3D, Ireland. (servicecentre@itgovernance.eu)